DEADLY DISEASES

INFLUENZA

BY KRISTINA LYN HEITKAMP

CONTENT CONSULTANT
Aubree Gordon, PhD
Associate Professor of Epidemiology
University of Michigan School of Public Health

Cover image: Structures called spikes on the surface of the
influenza virus help it enter host cells.

Core Library

An Imprint of Abdo Publishing
abdobooks.com

abdobooks.com

Published by Abdo Publishing, a division of ABDO, PO Box 398166, Minneapolis, Minnesota 55439. Copyright © 2022 by Abdo Consulting Group, Inc. International copyrights reserved in all countries. No part of this book may be reproduced in any form without written permission from the publisher. Core Library™ is a trademark and logo of Abdo Publishing.

Printed in the United States of America, North Mankato, Minnesota.
102021
012022

THIS BOOK CONTAINS
RECYCLED MATERIALS

Cover Photo: Shutterstock Images
Interior Photos: National Archives and Records Administration/Science Source, 4–5, 16, 43; Natalia Lisovskaya/Shutterstock Images, 8; Diego Cervo/Shutterstock Images, 10; German Vizulis/ Shutterstock Images, 12–13; Everett Collection/Shutterstock Images, 14; AP Images, 18; Red Line Editorial, 21, 26; CNRI/Science Source, 24–25, 45; Studio Romantic/Shutterstock Images, 29; Drazen Zigic/Shutterstock Images, 31; Syda Productions/Shutterstock Images, 34–35; Joe Raedle/Getty Images News/Getty Images, 37; Wally Santana/AP Images, 38

Editor: Arnold Ringstad
Series Designer: Ryan Gale

Library of Congress Control Number: 2021941247

Publisher's Cataloging-in-Publication Data

Names: Heitkamp, Kristina Lyn, author.
Title: Influenza / by Kristina Lyn Heitkamp
Description: Minneapolis, Minnesota : Abdo Publishing, 2022 | Series: Deadly diseases | Includes online resources and index.
Identifiers: ISBN 9781532196591 (lib. bdg.) | ISBN 9781098218409 (ebook)
Subjects: LCSH: Influenza--Juvenile literature. | Influenza viruses--Juvenile literature. | Infectious diseases--Juvenile literature. | Epidemics--History--Juvenile literature. | Communicable diseases--Epidemiology--Juvenile literature.
Classification: DDC 614.49--dc23

CONTENTS

SURVIVING A DEADLY VIRUS

S adie Afraid of His Horses was only seven years old when her family survived a deadly influenza pandemic. Her father was an important Oglala Sioux leader. Sadie and her family lived in South Dakota on the Pine Ridge Indian Reservation.

In September 1918, Sadie and her family were in Nebraska. They were harvesting potatoes to earn money. Her aunts, uncles, cousins, grandmother, and great-grandmother all worked.

The influenza pandemic of 1918 spread to nearly every corner of the world.

NEWS OF SICKNESS

The family heard that a very bad sickness was spreading. People said they should go back home to South Dakota. Sadie was nervous and a bit scared. She had already seen many wagons taking people who had died from influenza to the graveyard. Plus, the family heard the sickness had reached the reservation. They packed up their wagons and headed home.

It was a five-day journey back to South Dakota. Sadie's cousin Edgar usually drove the wagon. But he was sick. Instead, her grandmother, Nancy Poor-Elk Red Cloud, steered the horses. Along the way, they hit bad weather. Also, more of the family caught the flu. Luckily, a farmer in Nebraska said they could stay with him until the rain stopped.

SWEETGRASS AND CEDAR TEA

Sadie's grandmother took charge. She told everyone to isolate in their tents. Family members who were sick stayed in separate tents. Sadie's grandmother brought food and medicine to all of them, and she made sure nobody shared cups, washbasins, or forks. Influenza caused fever, horrible coughing, and tiredness. She made cedar tea for them to drink. She burned sweetgrass in hopes of helping them breathe better. She rubbed a lotion on their foreheads to help bring the fever down.

PERSPECTIVES

NEWSPAPER ACCOUNTS

In 1918, people did not know what caused the influenza pandemic or how it spread. Newspaper reports from the time tried to make sense of what was happening. A July 1918 story from the *Salt Lake Telegram* said, "The [flu] plague seems to have no system in spreading itself. It jumps from one country to another, over seas and mountains. . . . In the present epidemic it has jumped France and the English Channel to England."

The entire family survived. They continued their journey home. Grandmother Nancy Poor-Elk Red Cloud's treatment helped save her family. Sadie lived until she was 99 years old. Her family said that she kept

People from some Native American cultures burn sweetgrass as part of ceremonies.

her medicine bag stocked with cedar and sweetgrass. She never complained when she was sick and would often treat her minor illnesses herself.

FIGHTING THE INFECTION

Sadie and her family survived the terrible influenza pandemic of 1918. But about 50 to 100 million people around the world weren't as lucky. This death toll made it one of the deadliest pandemics in history. The disease was highly contagious. It quickly spread everywhere, even to the Alaskan wilderness and remote Pacific islands. In the most severe cases, the virus caused the lungs to fill with fluid and the skin to turn blue.

1918 INFLUENZA OR THE SPANISH FLU?

The 1918 influenza is sometimes called the Spanish flu. That name makes it sound like the virus started in Spain. But this might not be true. The outbreak began during World War I (1914–1918). The warring governments kept stories about the outbreak out of their newspapers. But Spain was not involved in the war. The Spanish media published stories of the influenza virus. When the news finally reached the rest of the world, it was from Spanish sources. The exact origin of the deadly virus is still unknown.

This worldwide disaster was caused by something too small to see. The influenza virus infects the nose, throat, and lungs. It spreads through tiny

droplets created by sneezing, coughing, or talking. It causes the disease influenza, also known as the flu.

Today, vaccines can help prevent people from getting the flu. However, new variants of the virus continue to appear. Doctors and scientists study and track these variants. None have been as deadly as the 1918 flu, but experts agree that it is important to be watchful to prevent another flu pandemic.

FURTHER EVIDENCE

Chapter One shares a story of a family who survived the deadly 1918 influenza. Identify the main points of this chapter and write down evidence supporting them. Then, visit the website below. Does the information on the website support the main point of the chapter? Does it present new evidence?

SOCIAL DISTANCING DURING A PANDEMIC

abdocorelibrary.com/influenza

Each year millions of people around the world are infected with influenza.

THE HISTORY
OF INFLUENZA

I t's hard to pinpoint when the influenza virus first appeared. Some records suggest that the virus has been around for a long time. A flu-like virus was described by the Greek physician Hippocrates around 410 BCE. Later reports of possible influenza outbreaks were recorded in the 1100s and 1500s CE. One of the earliest likely pandemics happened in 1580. It began in Russia and spread to Europe and the Americas.

Hippocrates is sometimes called the "father of medicine."

The 1918 pandemic spread widely among soldiers during World War I.

THE 1918 PANDEMIC

The influenza pandemic of 1918 was one of the deadliest disease outbreaks ever. The flu infected up to one-third of the world's population. It spread quickly and mostly affected healthy people 15 to 34 years old. Many of them died. The virus weakened the lungs and led to severe infections. But there were no effective medicines to treat the disease and its symptoms.

More soldiers died from influenza than were killed in World War I (1914–1918). Historians think that the war contributed to the spread of the virus. Soldiers traveled in large groups. They often stayed in crowded army camps. The flu vaccine had not been invented yet. Doctors tried everything to treat the virus. Some said eating cinnamon or oranges would help.

Governments tried to slow the disease's spread. Health departments told the public not to touch library books. Some schools, churches, and theaters closed. A few towns even shut themselves off from other towns. Some cities required everyone to wear a face mask. Those who refused faced punishments, such as fines or jail time.

By the summer of 1920, the pandemic was fading away. Tens of millions of people had died. About 675,000 of those deaths were in the United States.

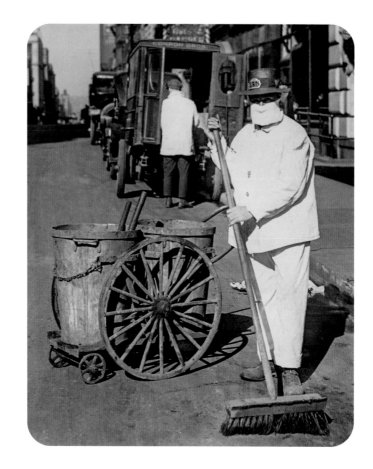

Many people wore face masks to slow the spread of the 1918 flu pandemic.

THE VIRUS CONTINUES

Since the deadly pandemic of 1918, the world has faced other dangerous outbreaks of flu. These included pandemics in 1957, 1968, and 2009. None were as deadly as the 1918 flu. Still, many people lost their lives. During this period, experts continued to learn more about the virus and how to manage an outbreak.

In 1957 a new influenza virus surfaced in East Asia. It started in southwestern China. Then it spread to Singapore and Hong Kong. It reached the United States by June. Symptoms included a sore throat, wobbly legs, and a high fever.

The 1957–1958 influenza virus killed more than one million people worldwide. That included more than 100,000 in the United States. More may have died if not for virologist Maurice Hilleman.

HISTORY OF THE INFLUENZA VACCINE

Influenza vaccines have two main goals: to protect against the virus and to keep it from spreading. The first influenza vaccine was created in the 1940s. Researchers used fertilized chicken eggs to grow the viruses used in the vaccines. This method is still used today. The first flu vaccine was given to soldiers fighting in World War II (1939–1945). By 1960 doctors started recommending that elderly and high-risk groups get a flu shot every year. But as the influenza virus evolved and changed, so did the vaccine. To keep the vaccine effective, scientists continue to make changes.

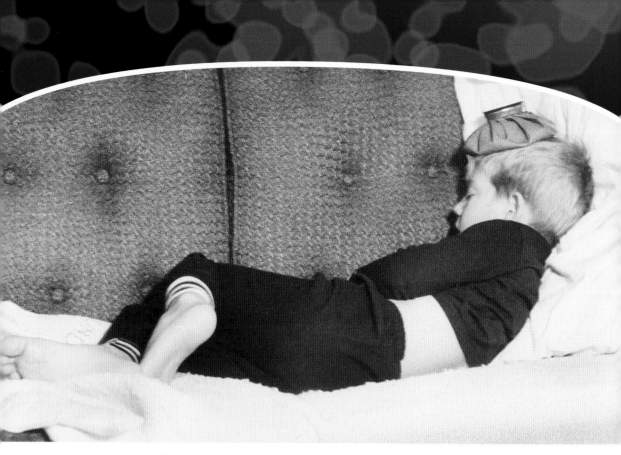

The 1968 influenza pandemic infected many thousands of people in the United States.

He heard about the outbreak in Asia. To help, he developed a vaccine and made it available in just a few months. The vaccine saved thousands of lives.

A decade later, another new influenza virus popped up in Hong Kong. The flu of 1968 was very contagious. It caused weakness, muscle pain, and fever. Scientists think the 1968 flu evolved from the 1957 flu. It mostly affected infants and the elderly. But some people who had been exposed to the 1957 flu seemed immune to the 1968 flu. A variation of the 1968 flu continues to spread each year during flu season.

THE 1976 OUTBREAK

In 1976 a new influenza virus broke out on a military base in New Jersey. It seemed to spread quickly from person to person. Some thought it might be like the 1918 influenza. The 1976 virus hadn't infected anybody outside of the military base yet. So, authorities acted quickly.

President Gerald Ford launched a huge vaccination campaign. Within a few months, 40 million Americans were vaccinated. But in the end, a pandemic never happened. Nobody outside of the military base got sick. And the vaccine carried a small risk of causing a rare nerve disorder. The disorder involves nerve damage, muscle weakness, and sometimes paralysis. The immunization program was stopped.

People criticized the government's response to the 1976 flu outbreak.

THE VIRUS HITS AGAIN

In the spring of 2009, scientists detected a new influenza virus in California. The 2009 influenza infected around 60 million Americans. Though it spread widely, the death toll was far lower than with other pandemics. It caused almost 13,000 deaths.

Again, some people who were exposed to the 1957 influenza showed immunity to the 2009 influenza.

2009 FLU HOSPITALIZATIONS
BY AGE

The 2009 influenza outbreak affected people of different ages differently. Older people were less severely affected than young people. The graphic below shows hospitalization rates for the 2009 flu by age groups. Why might flu outbreaks affect people of different ages differently?

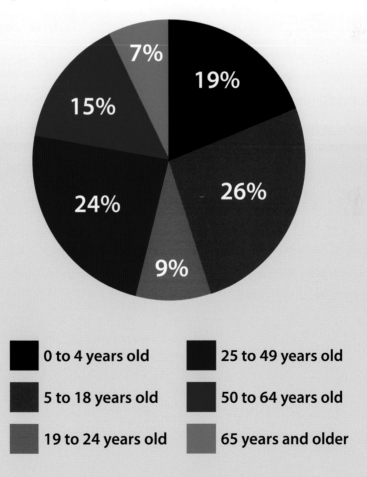

■ 0 to 4 years old	■ 25 to 49 years old
■ 5 to 18 years old	■ 50 to 64 years old
■ 19 to 24 years old	■ 65 years and older

With other influenza outbreaks, the spread slowed during the summer. But in 2009, summer infection rates were high. By June the flu had spread to 74 other countries. The virus spread through coughing or sneezing, and it most affected young, healthy people. Symptoms included headaches, a sore throat, and body aches.

Scientists developed a vaccine later that fall. By the summer of 2010, the pandemic had ended. But the 2009 flu virus is still around. It is one of the strains that cause seasonal flu.

STRAIGHT TO THE
SOURCE

The Red Cross placed the following advertisement in the *San Francisco Chronicle* during the 1918 pandemic:

Wear a mask and save your life! The emergency that now confronts our city is beyond the facilities of the health department. The Red Cross has come to the assistance of the Board of Health. Doctors and nurses can not be obtained to take care of the afflicted. You must wear a mask, not only to protect yourself but your children and your neighbor from influenza, pneumonia and death. A gauze mask is 99% proof against influenza. Doctors wear them. Those who do not wear them get sick. The man or woman or child who will not wear a mask is a dangerous slacker. Wear masks going to work, at work, going home, at home.

Source: Douglas Zimmerman. "San Francisco Forced People to Wear Masks during the 1918 Spanish Flu Pandemic. Did It Help?" *SF Gate*, 10 Apr. 2020, sfgate.com. Accessed 6 July 2021.

BACK IT UP

The author of this passage is using evidence to support a point. Write a paragraph describing the point the author is making. Then write down two or three pieces of evidence the author uses to make the point.

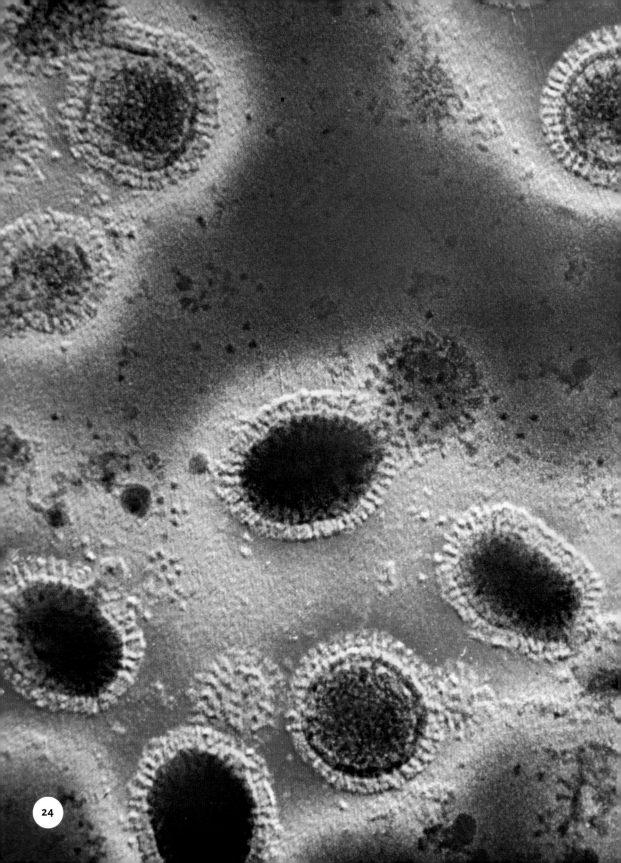

THE SCIENCE OF INFLUENZA

There are four types of influenza viruses: A, B, C, and D. Type A infects both animals and humans. It can infect chickens, pigs, and even horses. Type A viruses are the most dangerous. They can cause pandemics. The 1918 influenza was this type. Type B infects only humans. Type C usually causes mild sickness. Type D mainly affects cattle.

Scientists name a type A virus based on which protein sits on the surface of the virus.

Influenza viruses can be seen using powerful microscopes.

INFLUENZA
VIRUSES

Influenza Type A viruses can affect many different animals, including humans, birds, pigs, horses, and even cats. How does this graphic help you better understand the different kinds of influenza viruses?

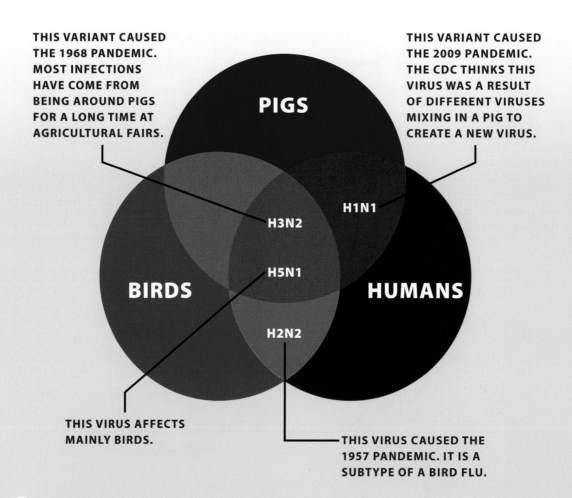

THIS VARIANT CAUSED THE 1968 PANDEMIC. MOST INFECTIONS HAVE COME FROM BEING AROUND PIGS FOR A LONG TIME AT AGRICULTURAL FAIRS.

THIS VARIANT CAUSED THE 2009 PANDEMIC. THE CDC THINKS THIS VIRUS WAS A RESULT OF DIFFERENT VIRUSES MIXING IN A PIG TO CREATE A NEW VIRUS.

PIGS

H1N1

H3N2

H5N1

BIRDS

HUMANS

H2N2

THIS VIRUS AFFECTS MAINLY BIRDS.

THIS VIRUS CAUSED THE 1957 PANDEMIC. IT IS A SUBTYPE OF A BIRD FLU.

The protein is either hemagglutinin (H) or neuraminidase (N). These proteins are called antigens. There are multiple kinds of both H and N. In all, there are 198 possible combinations for a type A virus. The 1957 flu was an H2N2. The 1968 flu was an H3N2. And the 2009 flu was an H1N1.

Sometimes the flu that makes a bird or pig sick can also make a human sick. This usually happens when a person comes into

DRIFTING AND SHIFTING

The influenza virus is always evolving. As it reproduces, the virus changes a little bit. These small changes add up. This is called antigenic drift. When this happens, the body's immune system may not recognize the changed virus. It will have a harder time fighting the virus. This is why a new influenza vaccine is needed each year. Influenza viruses can also change in big ways. This is called antigenic shift. It happens when two kinds of influenza viruses mix and make a new virus. For example, if a pig is infected with both pig and bird flu, a new mixed virus may form inside the pig. Scientists believe antigenic shift is how many pandemics began.

close contact with the sick animal. Humans have very rarely gotten sick from type A bird flu. When this does happen, the virus rarely spreads to another person. Type A swine flu is similar. Flu viruses that infect pigs usually do not infect humans. But when they do, they can mix to form new flu viruses. Pigs can carry not only swine viruses but also bird and human viruses. This mixing can be dangerous. It can create a new virus that starts a pandemic.

SEASONAL VERSUS PANDEMIC

Influenza viruses can result in seasonal flu or pandemic flu. Seasonal flu spreads each year. Pandemic flu is less common but can be more deadly. Both usually spread the same way. But a pandemic virus can infect and kill more people because it is new. Fewer people have immunity to it. The big flu events of 1918, 1957, 1968, and 2009 were all pandemic influenzas.

There is a vaccine for the seasonal flu. The vaccine is designed to protect against the most likely seasonal

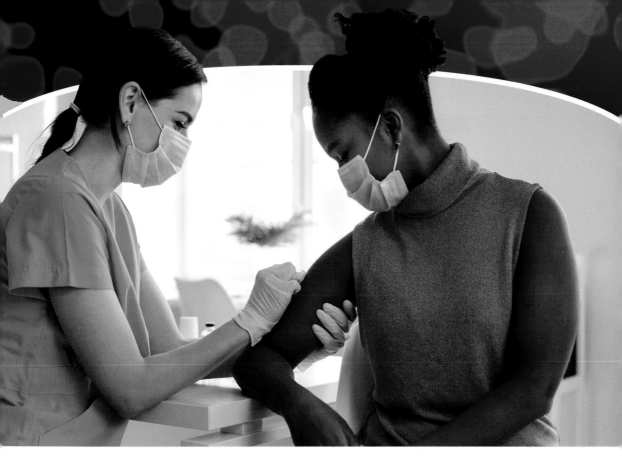

Health-care workers give out millions of vaccines against seasonal flu each year.

flus that year. But it is nearly impossible to predict a pandemic flu. There is no single vaccine that defends against all flus.

Figuring out who is most at risk from the flu is complicated. For example, the seasonal flu is usually most dangerous to older people. But the 2009 pandemic flu affected healthy young adults.

COVER YOUR COUGH

The influenza virus spreads in tiny droplets. When a sick person sneezes, coughs, or talks, these droplets spread. Other people may breathe in the droplets. Or the droplets may land on a surface, such as a book or a door handle. If a person touches that surface and then touches his or her mouth or nose, the person can become infected.

A person with influenza may start showing symptoms one to four days after becoming infected. Some people who are infected have no symptoms. This is called being asymptomatic. One in three people who get influenza are asymptomatic. Infected people may spread the virus a day before they start to feel sick. They can continue spreading it for about a week after the illness starts.

The first day of symptoms includes headaches or sleepiness. Then a dry cough or body aches and chills follow. Sometimes the flu can cause vomiting

Covering a cough or sneeze is a good way to avoid spreading viruses.

or diarrhea in kids, but this is not typical. The flu is a respiratory virus. It mainly affects the nose, lungs, and throat.

The flu usually enters the body through the nose or mouth. Once inside the nose, the virus infects cells in the nose. From there, the virus makes copies of itself and continues infecting other cells. When the body's immune system notices the infection, it fights the invading viruses. An achy body and headache are signs that the body is working to kill infected cells.

STRAIGHT TO THE
SOURCE

Dr. Anthony Fauci is the head of the National Institute of Allergy and Infectious Diseases. In a 2020 interview, he talked about the creation of flu vaccines in 2009:

> *We started seeing widespread cases of H1N1 in the spring of 2009 and we were able to make a vaccine against it. But when the fall came, even though we had a vaccine for both H3N2 and H1N1, the H1N1 virus completely dominated the season and kicked the anticipated seasonal H3N2 off the map. Luckily, H1N1, although it was pervasive in transmission, it was kind of a wimpy virus and the deaths that year were even less than a regular seasonal flu year.*

> Source: "A Conversation with Anthony S. Fauci, MD, on COVID-19 and Influenza." *American College of Cardiology,* 12 Aug. 2020, acc.org. Accessed 7 July 2021.

WHAT'S THE BIG IDEA?

Take a close look at this passage. What is Dr. Fauci saying about the challenges of creating vaccines for different kinds of influenza viruses?

TREATING INFLUENZA

The Centers for Disease Control and Prevention (CDC) is the US government agency responsible for public health. It estimates that between 12,000 and 61,000 people die from influenza each year. The influenza season is typically from late fall to spring. Most people recover from the flu without treatment. Usually all that is needed is rest and lots of fluids. Water, juice, or warm soups can help a sick person

People usually recover from a flu by resting and treating the symptoms.

stay hydrated. And sleep helps the immune system fight the infection. But some people develop problems, such as pneumonia. This sickness infects the lungs. It can be deadly. If severe symptoms happen, such as a high fever or difficulty breathing, experts say people should get help right away.

The CDC says the best way to prevent seasonal flu is to get the vaccine. Two common forms of the influenza vaccine are a shot and a nasal spray. The shot is given with a needle into the arm. There are many different variations of the flu shot. The nasal spray is sprayed into the nose. There are several limits on who should get the spray. For example, it is not recommended for those with asthma or adults over 50 years old.

Influenza vaccines are made and updated each year. The virus constantly evolves and changes. Experts say everyone six months old and older should get the annual vaccine. Each year the vaccine is made based on

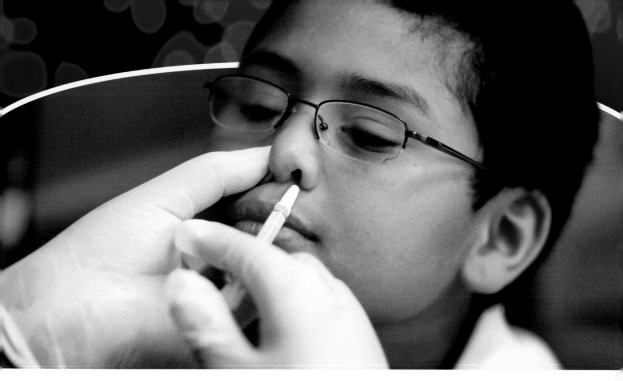

A nasal spray is one typical way of receiving a flu vaccine.

research collected from many places and people. During the year, researchers from all over the world study different influenza viruses. They gather information about which viruses are spreading. These scientists share what they learn with top world health experts. Hospitals also report their discoveries. All of this information helps scientists design the annual vaccine.

CHALLENGES FOR THE VACCINE

Although the vaccine prevents millions of people from getting sick, it does face challenges. The effectiveness

Scientists around the world study new and improved flu vaccines.

of the vaccine varies. It can work about 40 percent to 60 percent of the time. This is because it is difficult to match a vaccine to flu viruses. Also, some people forget to get the vaccine or don't want to get it.

To solve some of these problems, scientists are studying a possible universal influenza vaccine. This is a shot that would protect against all kinds of flu viruses. Scientists would no longer have to match the vaccine to the virus. Early tests of a universal vaccine began in 2021. If it works, it could change the way doctors fight the flu.

Another challenge facing the vaccine is misinformation. For example, some people think that flu shots cause the flu. But this is not the case. These shots are made with either inactive viruses or only one small part from the virus. They cannot cause the flu. Another myth is that healthy people don't need to get vaccinated. But a flu infection can cause serious issues even for healthy people. If people believe these myths, they may choose not to get vaccinated.

PREVENTING COVID-19 AND INFLUENZA

During the flu season of 2020–2021, the World Health Organization reported record low numbers of influenza cases. Scientists think it was because the public was busy fighting COVID-19. People were wearing masks, social distancing, and working and learning remotely. Influenza viruses are transmitted the same way as the coronavirus that causes COVID-19. Medical centers busy with COVID-19 cases reported fewer or no flu hospitalizations. In the previous flu season, there had been 22,000 deaths. In the 2020–2021 season, there were just 700.

STOPPING THE SPREAD

The CDC says that to help control the spread of influenza, people should stay home if they're feeling sick. Other tips include covering coughs and sneezes with a tissue. Washing hands helps too. If soap and water aren't available, the CDC says to use an alcohol-based hand sanitizer. It also says to avoid touching your eyes, nose, and mouth.

In 2005 the US Department of Health

and Human Services (HHS) developed a Pandemic Influenza Plan. It includes tools and tips to prevent, control, and respond to a pandemic flu outbreak. But preparing for an influenza pandemic is an ongoing task. Scientists continue to study the 1918 influenza virus. Researchers also keep an eye on the different influenzas that affect animals. Health officials continue to update the plan. By being prepared, they hope to stop the next deadly flu pandemic before it starts.

EXPLORE ONLINE

Chapter Four talks about how to prevent the spread of influenza. The website below discusses how to avoid spreading COVID-19, which is also a respiratory virus. How is the information from the website the same as the information in Chapter Four? How is it different?

HELP STOP THE SPREAD OF CORONAVIRUS AND PROTECT YOUR FAMILY

abdocorelibrary.com/influenza

IMPORTANT DATES

Around 410 BCE
The Greek doctor Hippocrates writes about a sickness similar to what we now know as the flu.

1918
An influenza pandemic kills tens of millions of people around the world.

1940s
Scientists create the first influenza vaccine using fertilized chicken eggs. The first people to get the vaccine are soldiers fighting in World War II.

1957
The 1957 influenza pandemic kills more than one million people worldwide.

1968
First discovered in the United States, the 1968 influenza mostly affects elderly people.

1976

A new flu outbreak happens on a military base in the United States. The government gives 40 million people vaccines in case it becomes a pandemic flu, but it never does.

2005

The US Department of Health and Human Services develops a Pandemic Influenza Plan. The plan includes strategies and methods to respond to a pandemic flu outbreak.

2009

The 2009 influenza virus infects about 60 million Americans, along with millions of other people around the globe.

2020

As a result of steps taken during the COVID-19 pandemic, flu cases in the 2020–2021 flu season drop sharply.

STOP AND
THINK

Surprise Me

Chapter Three discusses the science behind influenza. After reading this book, what two or three facts about influenza did you find most surprising? Write a few sentences about each fact. Why did you find each fact surprising?

Say What?

Studying science and medicine can mean learning a lot of new vocabulary. Find five words in this book you've never heard before. Use a dictionary to find out what they mean. Then write the meanings in your own words and use each word in a new sentence.

Take a Stand

The CDC says the best way to prevent the flu is to get the vaccine. But some people don't think they need the flu shot because they are healthy. How would you convince someone that getting a flu shot is still important?

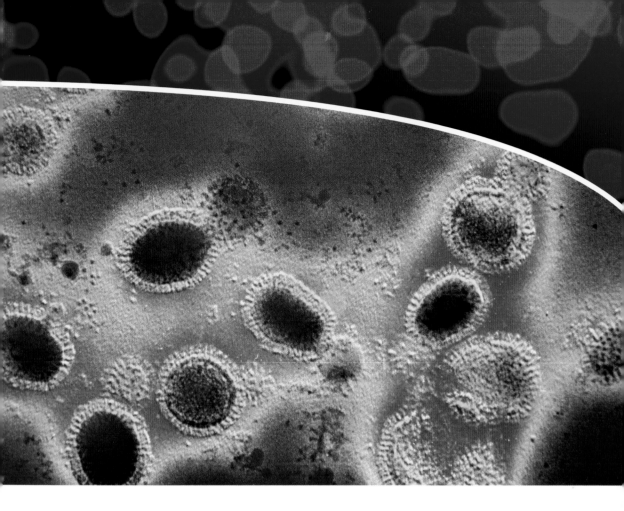

You Are There

This book discusses the steps people took to slow the spread of the 1918 influenza pandemic. Many of those steps are similar to what people did during the COVID-19 pandemic. Imagine you can travel back in time and talk to a person who lived through the 1918 pandemic. How would you explain the COVID-19 pandemic to them? What would you ask them about the 1918 pandemic?

GLOSSARY

antigen
a substance that triggers the immune system to fight an infection

asymptomatic
to be sick but not have any symptoms

contagious
able to spread a sickness

hygiene
the practice of keeping yourself clean

immune system
the body's network of cells, tissues, and organs that help fight infection and disease

misinformation
false information

pandemic
the spread of a disease in many countries

pneumonia
an infection in the lungs that makes it hard to breathe

protein
a category of complex substances found in living things

vaccine
a medicine given to people or animals to prevent them from getting sick and from spreading illness to others

virologist
a scientist who studies viruses

ONLINE RESOURCES

To learn more about influenza, visit our free resource websites below.

Visit **abdocorelibrary.com** or scan this QR code for free Common Core resources for teachers and students, including vetted activities, multimedia, and booklinks, for deeper subject comprehension.

Visit **abdobooklinks.com** or scan this QR code for free additional online weblinks for further learning. These links are routinely monitored and updated to provide the most current information available.

LEARN MORE

Brown, Don. *Fever Year: The Killer Flu of 1918*. HMH Books, 2019.

Messner, Kate. *History Smashers: Plagues and Pandemics*. Random House Children's Books, 2021.

INDEX

About the Author

Kristina Lyn Heitkamp is a Utah-based children's book author and environmental journalist. She has written and edited more than 20 books and articles on many topics, including universal health care and medical 3D printing.